I0199118

Fish, Chips, Peas, then Apple-Pie Day

Poems by

Valerie Bell

STOCKWELL
PUBLISHERS SINCE 1898

Published in 2022 by
Valerie Bell
in association with
Arthur H Stockwell Ltd
West Wing Studios
Unit 166, The Mall
Luton, Bedfordshire
ahstockwell.co.uk

Copyright © 2022 Valerie Bell

The right of Valerie Bell to be identified as the author
of this work has been asserted in accordance with
the Copyright, Designs and Patents Act 1988.

All rights reserved. No reproduction, copy or transmission
of this publication may be made without express prior
written permission. No paragraph of this publication may be
reproduced, copied or transmitted except with express prior
written permission or in accordance with the provisions of the
Copyright Act 1956 (as amended). Any person who commits
any unauthorised act in relation to this publication may be
liable to criminal prosecution and civil claims for damage.

British Library Cataloguing-in-Publication Data:
A catalogue record for this book is
available from the British Library.
ISBN 9780722351468

The views and opinions expressed within this
book belong to the author and do not necessarily
reflect those of the Arthur H Stockwell Ltd.

Dedicated to Kevin, and Paul, for their love, inspiration, and support, but most of all, their ears.

Thank you both. XX

Contents

Fish, Chips, Peas, then Apple-Pie Day

Chaos Theory

I went for a walk as I needed some air,
I'd a head full of damp cotton wool.
I didn't know why – there'd been no bad news,
so nothing had happened to bring on the blues,
and the booze bottle's still pretty full.

For a time things went well as I trotted along,
enjoying the birds in the trees.
The breeze was quite fresh, and the flowers in bloom,
a beautiful day full of nature's perfume,
then the pain struck in both of me knees.

It didn't half hurt, coming on all at once,
just out of the blue with no warning.
Lucky for me, I was quite near a seat,
so I staggered and shuffled the final few feet,—
what a start to a beautiful morning!

I massaged and rubbed my rheumaticky joints,
to try and get ease from the pain.
It did little good, but what else could I do?—
and till the pain passed, I would look at the view,
then set off on my trek once again.

Eventually I made it back on to my feet,
and hobbled my way towards home.
I'd started out feeling as joyful as Spring;
now all I felt fit for, was the nearest dustbin,
boy, was I going to have a good moan!

Because I was slow, it took me some time,
which did nothing to help my bad mood.
And when I got through the door, I was ready to curse,
cos my glasses steamed up – things were just getting worse;
now I was going to have to be rude.

And I would've, if I'd not stumbled over the cat,
who was disturbed by me making a fuss.
He then cleared off so quick,
at a helluva lick,
and can shift when he wants to, that puss.

Any road up – I had now had enough,
but fate hadn't finished her fun,
as the urge we all know when you're needing the loo,
and you can't get the knot out the lace of your shoe,
came on me – and I started to run.

What a mistake! I should never have tried,
but my bladder was ready to burst.
I pulled off my glasses, as the mist was still there,
and went flat out, and winded, across the hall chair,
so I cursed, and I cursed, and I cursed.

Lucky for me, the wife had gone out,
so she'd have no idea what I'd done.
And I wouldn't tell her, and nor would the cat,
for I knew from the past that the cat wouldn't rat.
His priority? Himself – number one.

I got to the loo, with just seconds to spare,
and gave thanks for small mercies received;
after washing my hands I went back to the hall,
where I straightened things up, leaving no trace at all,
of the gymnastics that I'd just achieved.

A proper sit-down with a nice cup of tea's—
what I needed, 'n' had definitely earned.
My knees were still creaky – rheumatics a curse,
but I had to remember, it could always be worse.
This was something from life I had learned.

No further mishaps occurred as I worked,—
on this precious and lifesaving brew;
then with two chocolate Hobnobs, fig roll and a Twix,
a little unusual, but a very nice mix,
I sat down, and thought my day through.

Though not given to dwelling on negative things
I mused on what else could go wrong,
and I found out that instant, as I picked up the tea,
cos the blasted stuff spilt, on the brand-new settee,
now there *was* going to be a ding-dong.

It wasn't as if I liked my tea weak—
a real builder's brew was the best.
The sort that'd strip all the varnish off wood,
and if it melted the spoon, then it must've been good,
'n' I wouldn't have anything less.

Then just at that moment, fate took charge again,
as I heard the wife's key in the lock.
She was going to kill me, when she saw what I'd done,
and with my gammy knees, well, I just couldn't run,
so no chance of escape round the block.

Mopping like mad, in forlorn and vain hope,
of concealing the large dark-brown stain,
I wrung out my hankie back into the cup;
it would've been nice if I'd managed one sup.
How the hell was I going to explain!

It's been a while now, and the settee's had a clean.
you have to peer, to see the faint mark still there,
yet nothing I've tried, and nothing I've said,
has got me back into our marital bed,
so I'm living one lifelong nightmare.

Ghost in the Machine

'What the hell's wrong with this blasted machine?'
I thought as I gave it a tap.
A nicely aimed chuck, in the next nearest bin,
would be what it'd get, or a good hefty fling—
why didn't I just use a map?

A beefier prod had no better response,
so I gave up and had a good swear.
What to do next? Mmm, look for a pub!—
that's the idea: have some freshly cooked grub,
and I'm bound to find somebody there
who'll
help me with what, the Satnav could not,
cos there's always a local who'll know
every Tom, Dick and Harry, and others,
besides,
I might buy them a round to get them onside—
with directions I could easily follow.

A mile further on, and what did I find—
the answer to every man's prayer:
a pub that served food, and it looked pretty good.
a few cars in the park, so in all likelihood
I'd find what I wanted right there.

I got out of the car, and had a look round—
first impressions are always the best.
With no thumping music, or arguing shouts,
no screaming kids, or loud drunken louts,
now let's go put this place to the test.

On opening the door, a faint friendly buzz
came wafting its way to my ears.
I could see people eating, and yon side of the bar—
others enjoying a nice friendly jar.
Yes – the right place to wind down and say, "Cheers."

Food duly ordered – a pint in my hand,
so now to settle in and relax.
I saw what I needed tucked out of the way,
only one oldish bloke there – that was OK—
then I'd eat, and set about making tracks.

Nodding acknowledgement to the old man,
I sat myself down with a sigh.
What a really nice place – a welcoming fire—
a full-bodied beer – made me want to retire,—
what could possibly now go awry?

'Nothing,' I thought. 'It's all working out,'
after initially fearing the worst.
'Just sort out the client and earn a fat fee,—
give him a discount and a good guarantee.'
For a time there I thought I'd been cursed.

The old man cleared his throat, and gave me a start,
just as I got out my phone.
He shuffled about – sipped at his beer,
and in a wood-whiskey voice said, "You're a stranger round here."
God, I wish now I'd sat on my own!

The next twenty minutes passed by in a blur,
as he poured out his sad, woeful story.
A quiz show on the 'box's' what he'd appeared on.
He'd known every answer – yes, every damned one—
then some tarty mare'd stolen his glory.

Ten thousand quid, the prize up for grabs,
or twenty if you scored with the double.
But – she'd fake 'lashes and nails, blond hair 'n' bleached teeth,
'n' a halfwit could tell there was nowt underneath—
from the start you could see she was trouble!

He swore it was fixed – she was thick as a plank,
and could never have won playing fair.
It should've been him, coming home with the crown;
instead, all he'd got was a nervous breakdown,
and brought to the edge of despair.

With tears in his eyes, and a break in his voice,
he repeated, "It should've been me."
So all I could think, was to get him a drink,
and, when I got there, tip the barman the wink,
cos the old chap needed help, I could see.

I paid for the whisky, and with a shrug of my head
I commented on the old guy.
The barman looked up, and went a bit green,
then stared in my eyes and said, "What you've just seen
is the ghost of the old Benjamin Fry!"

Now, I'm not a soft sod – I stand my own ground,
but the blood drained down straight to my feet.
I looked round the room; the old man wasn't there—
he'd've had to walk past me to get anywhere,
and there was nobody there in that seat!

"You're pulling my leg – you're having me on!"
my voice came out just a bit loud.
"No joke," said the barman with shock on his face.
"Last time he came in, – he died in that place."
By now we were drawing a crowd.

"The stress was too much," croaked the barman again,
"he never behaved the same way.
It ate at his soul – he just couldn't cope,
then it got to the stage where he gave up all hope,
but we thought he would rally one day."

So I knocked back the whisky, – walked out of the pub,
'n' escaped from that spirit-soaked joint,—
gunned up the car, – put it in gear,
drove like the devil in sheer-naked fear,
and arrived at my own tipping point.

Invisible

"Hey! What in the hell are you shouting about?
I just couldn't help it – the old bat walked out!
The stupid fat cow came on into the road—
I couldn't've missed her – I'm sure I'd've slowed.
So what was she thinking, the daft dozy mare?
My new car's all dented – it's not bloody fair."

Her life – a sad story, devoid of much light.
It hadn't been easy,
and often the fight, had given her thoughts
that were too much to bear,
so she'd long since stopped thinking
of saying a prayer, for aid from above to help carry the load—
laid square on her shoulders; and now newly widowed,
she had gotten her freedom from dull, dreary drudge,
with no one at home now to moan,
or begrudge, a treat she had earned,
even though it be small,
it was hers to delight in, with no guilt at all.

But life it was funny, for now on her own;
what few friends she'd had, they all left her alone.
She phoned, and invited, or talked of a trip,
but they were too busy.
it seems the friendship, was subject to having a husband in tow.
Were they too embarrassed?—
or perhaps didn't know—
how to deal with the state she now found herself in,
though they'd claimed they'd be with her
through thick and through thin.
So she filled in her time just as best as she could,
coming to terms with this new widowhood.

Hairdressers, library, the shops and then park,
her house simply shone—
as not one fingermark, ever tainted a surface,
and no trace of dust, was allowed now to settle,—
Mr. Sheen was a must—
her very best friend, who would not let her down,
as he gave her a reason to go into town,
where she'd shop round in Savers and Asda,
or any, and all supermarkets,
to save just one penny.

Yet this feeling of triumph, it soon slipped away,
and the pleasure of saving, turned now to dismay,
as it dawned on her, nobody looked at her face;
they just thrust out their hand, and stared straight into space,
demanding her money, yet not seeing her there,
it was patently clear they did not even care.
From one place to another, and not ever being seen,
it happened so often
it was now all routine, to go through the day,
without barely a word, being exchanged with one person—
not ever being heard.

But she tried to persist and maintain a good heart,
even when her emotions were falling apart.
She found a new pastime to help her to mend,
so went to the bingo
and made a new friend, who just like herself
was alone and afraid,
and whose life, as with hers, was too heavily weighed
on passing the time,
as HER friends had moved on,
leaving HER also feeling
she didn't belong, in society
where being a pair, was the norm.
Where you didn't exist if you didn't conform.

The friendship it strengthened; brought change with new hopes,
for they shared not just bingo, but a love of the 'soaps'.
They both had new purpose, and days weren't so dull,
in fact, you could say they were pleasantly full.
But outside their world, mankind didn't change much,
still with sparse interaction, and scant human touch.

Then one summer's day, not a cloud in the sky,
life's course changed again
and one would now cry—
for the loss of her friend,
who when crossing the street
met the drug-fuelled aggression, of a loathsome deadbeat.
His Mummy and Daddy had bought him a car;
he'd at last passed his test – he was their little Star.
but what they didn't know about their precious child,
was when out of their sight, he ran feral and wild.

Now as she lay dying, her life in the gutter,
no-one would now hear the last sigh she would utter,
for they stood and took pictures
on a hand-held device,
with their senses long frozen, and hearts cold as ice,
as what they observed wasn't living or real,
it was all like a game, just remote and surreal.
Unseen she'd become once her husband had died;
unseen she'd remained when she ventured outside.

No one could now tell what had happened that day,
because they never saw,
so they just couldn't say, if she checked on the road,
or she simply stepped out,
and what, anyway, was the fuss all about?—
people died every day,
so what was one person more?
Just a batty old woman
who'd been shoved through death's door!

Tomorrow Always Comes

I wish I could remember just what day it is today.
I've wracked my brain, yet can't work out—
which one it is, but there's no doubt
when I do I'll say one blooming big hooray!

But worrying and fretting will not help to clear the mist.
I must not panic – just stay calm,
don't get worked up – that'd do more harm,
or the wretched problem really will persist.

A snort of oil of rosemary often clears the mental fuzz,
to sort the thoughts – to ease the mind,
to soothe things down, and help unwind—
at least I'm pretty sure that's what it does.

I've tried to keep a journal of the things I do, and when,
and look to check the tasks I've done
then not repeat a single one,
but I lost it – and had to do them all again.

And then a light-bulb moment flashed its way into my head:
an age-old trick that works a treat—
remember days by what you eat,
'n' if nothing else you'll know that you've been fed.

On paper the idea was good; in practice just one flaw,
and that involved a shopping list,
which I'd forget, and here's the twist:
it'd mean a second visit to the store.

So, I've given up – I do not care, whatever day it is.
Monday – Wednesday, let it go.
Tuesday – Thursday, I don't know.
But Friday – that is my day,
Fish, chips, peas, then apple-pie day,
and the good thing is,
I do it all again tomorrow.

Santa's Dilemma

Santa was fed up, and Santa was sick
of having to work every day—
to make all the presents, for spoilt selfish brats,
who treated him worse than a tatty doormat,
for they expected to get their own way.

Whatever they wanted, they believed they should have,
no matter the charge or the cost.
Their tantrums, their tempers, their sulks and their tears,
had hardened his heart over infinite years,
and the kindness once felt, he'd now lost.

So he pondered and thought, and he mulled and he mused,
on how he could right all this strife.
It wouldn't be easy – he knew that for sure,
and whatever the outcome, he'd have to endure—
the result, for the rest of his life.

He couldn't expect any help from the elves,
with the problem he now had to solve,
as they were too busy just packing the toys,
for bossyboot girls, and snotty-nosed boys.
This was going to be hard to resolve.

The first thing he did was to talk with a friend—
this was someone he'd known for some years.
He poured out his heart, and his soul, and his thoughts—
of how he felt weary, and right out of sorts,
and sometimes had shed a few tears.

But Rudolph, who was having an off day himself,
didn't want to seem cruel or unkind,
so he nodded and snuffled,
and snuzzled his muzzle, into Santa's soft shoulder,
taking care not to ruffle his red suit,
as he'd just had it ironed.

Well, this was a problem, of that there's no doubt,
with our special pair down in the dumps.
What would revive them, and make them feel good—
as they had been before, and still probably could—
as opposed to being grouchy old grumps?

Things weren't looking good, as they sat side by side
in the barn, where the reindeer all slept.
Santa was perched on his old wooden stool,
and Rudolph the floor, or he'd look such a fool,
and anyway, it was recently swept.

They looked at each other, and then looked around,
in hope of divine inspiration.
But nothing was happening to help with their quest,
and Santa was getting increasingly stressed.
and Rudolph could sense that frustration.

They highed and they sighed, and they puffed and they blowed,
yet nothing was coming to mind,
and Santa was starting to feel proper glum,
as the hard wooden stool – well, it made his bum numb.
What he'd give to have one that's fur-lined!

Now things had gone quiet, with no sounds around,
and Santa fell into a snooze.
Rudolph was resting his tired fuzzled head
on a bundle of straw, that would make a nice bed,
and they both drifted off in a muse.

It was a 'hoot-hooty-hoot-hoot' that made them both jump,
as an owl poked his head round the door.
He gave them a look, as if to say, "Hey,
it's in here, of all places, you're hiding away,
and I swear I heard one of you snore."

Both Santa and Rudolph had the grace now to blush,
and then dragged themselves out of their droop.
It was no good just moping and drifting away—
"Let's be up now and at 'em, no time for delay,"
or they really would be in the soup.

But just as they started being 'at 'em and up',
Mr. Owl stopped them there where they stood.
He asked what it was they were planning to do,
and, being a wise soul, he knew they had no clue,
but he'd help if he possibly could.

So Santa told Owly about his sad tale,
and of how he felt very much used.
Mr. Owl, he just nodded, not saying a word,
for he knew to keep quiet, that clever old bird,
when someone felt hurt and confused.

He also knew Rudolph, as Santa's good friend,
would want a solution found soon,
as Christmas was coming, and he and his team
would need to deliver, each and every child's dream,
and its an awfully long way round the moon.

This, then, was the way Mr. Owl sorted out,
the conundrum that Santa was in.
He explained that the children weren't selfish or spoilt,
they were just so excited – were wound up, and coiled,
like a super-strength, big bouncy spring.

For they loved to see Santa and Rudolph each year,
when they'd visit a nearby grotto.
It was something so special, but they couldn't express
their thoughts and their feelings – AND – barely suppress,
their delight at a new Christmas panto.

But children should also be taught from the start
that politeness, it goes a long way.
Tantrums and screaming are not very nice,
and should not be indulged in, – was Hooty's advice;
and if they did that, then they'd be OK.

So when he had finished he gave them a nod,
as if to say, "Now that you know,
you won't be upset, when the children get fraught.
for you'll see that they're tired, and much overwrought,
and I bet they'll be wishing for snow."

With that being all done, Hooty Owl hooted off,
for he'd done his good deed of the day.
Then Santa eyed Rudolph, and Rudolph looked back—
they were both feeling silly, and much taken aback.
Now they'd better go 'n' service the sleigh.

It was later that evening, when Santa relaxed,
whilst sitting in front of the fire.
As he slurped on his cocoa, and nibbled a cake,
he remembered his grumps, and it made his heart ache,
and he wondered if he should retire.

The words of dear Hooty still rang in his head,
and he felt such a deep sense of shame,
but the answer was not to give up, or give in—
he had to keep going through thick and through thin,
and Rudolph, he knew, felt the same.

He'd learned, being a hard-working man for some years,
and likewise the Dads and the Mums,
that sometimes the stresses and strains of the job,
can upset all your feelings, and make your head throb,
and put you deep down in the glums.

The cocoa worked wonders, and so did the cake,
and a restful night's sleep did the rest.
Santa was happy, and so were his crew—
he was bringing a Christmas for each one of you,
and with that, he felt joyous and blest.